The Parkinson Poems

To Judy, who, I understand, has great energy and heart for

The Parkinson Poems

JAN SEALE

Jan Seale

LAMAR UNIVERSITY PRESS

ISBN: 978-0-9850838-7-8
Library of Congress Control Number: 2013954488
Manufactured in the United States of America

Photography and Cover Design: Erren Seale

Lamar University Press
Beaumont, Texas

for Carl

Acknowledgments

Special thanks to our sons and their families for journeying with us; likewise to friends, doctors and caregivers; gratitude to the editors of Lamar University Press for believing in and implementing this unusual project; and appreciation to the National Parkinson Foundation, the Michael J. Fox Foundation, and the American Parkinson Disease Association for their widespread efforts of support, information, and research.

"Faces in Everything" first appeared in *Concho River Review*. "Dear Dr. Parkinson" and "Prey and Predator" were published in *Langdon Review of the Arts in Texas 2012-13*.

CONTENTS

The trouble with a chronic disease
is that it is...so...well...
chronic.

ONSET

No man alive can say, This shall not happen to me.
—Menander
(4th Century B.C.)

The Guest

I.
He came one day to the door,
knocked insistently
until they answered.
He begged to come in.
The husband said he wasn't there.
The wife thought she'd seen him earlier.
He proceeded to camp on the porch,
sprawled and made noises.
They couldn't go in or out
without noticing this guy.
Then one day it was too much.
The doctor gave the answer—
His name was Parkinson
and his presence was permanent.
With no choice, they opened the door.

II.
He darted past the doorkeeper,
unpacked a large satchel of gear,
announced he preferred
sleeping in the master bedroom.
He hung up his clothes
wrong side out.
All night he flounced, flopped,
made snorkeling noises,
breathed heavily.
They gave him the ground rules:
He'd have to stay home
when they went out.
He'd have to get lost
when they made love.
He was not
to interrupt conversations.
Know: they were moving on
with their lives despite him.

III.
For a while things went well—
at least in public.
The guest remained out of sight.
Friends said, "What guest?
You don't look any the worse for him."
But at home they had to step around
the naked mannequin he'd brought in—
the one with an unsmiling face
and arms that neither moved
nor could be detached.
He insisted on coming to table with them.
Soon, he wouldn't allow conversation
unless it was about him.
He dropped silverware, knocked over glasses,
spilt food, complained of dull knives,
awkward fork tines, spoons purposely small.
The meat was too tough to cut or chew.
Vegetables played tag all over the plate.
Lettuce salads intentionally went straight for the lap.
Tacos exploded; sandwiches dribbled and drooped.
Gradually, he began running the show.

IV.
He became the conversation director,
insisting they discuss him at least
several times a day—
discuss his strength, how complicated
his presence had become,
how they could get around the difficulties,
what they could do for him.
Other times, he asked them to drop
the conversation entirely,
for the man was too tired to talk,
or he didn't understand,
or the woman didn't understand—
or even if the man did,
and was even delighted,
he answered with silence
and what her limbic brain
signaled was a frown.
It was confusing.

V.

One day he said he'd taken a fancy
to go out with them,
for it was getting dull at home.
He rode in the back seat
but insisted the wife drive all the time.
He went everywhere with them
but wasn't interested in staying long.
In the middle of art galleries, parties,
dinner with friends, plays, concerts,
he asked to go home.
Home again, he stared at them
when they kissed goodnight,
and at dawn, he made it a habit
to call out loudly
with confrontations in dreams
that echoed through the house.

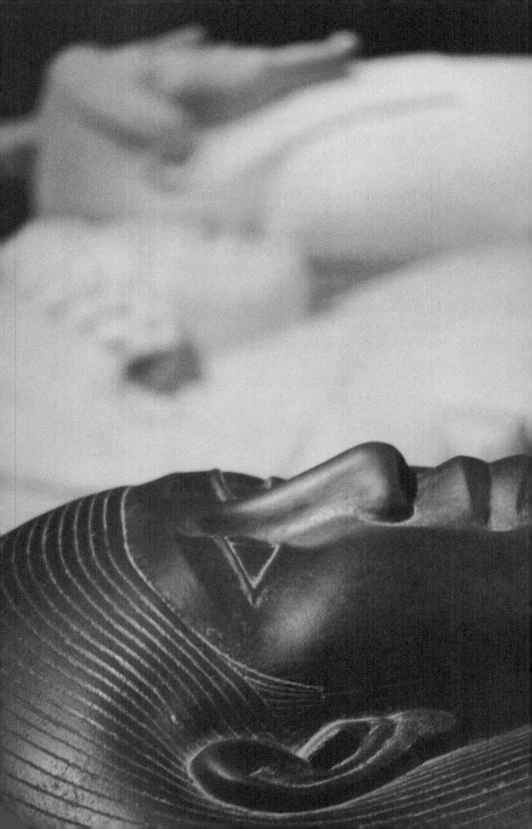

VI.
The guest now became the alpha dog.
By this time he had filled all the drawers
in the guest room,
had a key made for the front door,
subscribed to his favorite newspaper,
and started his mail there.
He was shopping for plants
to re-do the flower bed.
The principal fact: he had no plans to leave,
because he dearly loved the husband.
To prove it,
he provided socks hard to put on,
pants that wouldn't stay up,
shirts with difficult armholes,
strangling ties, lost handkerchiefs.

VII.
Time has passed and the guest
has added a new stipulation:
while he adores her husband,
enjoying such activities as brushing
his teeth in jumpy, ragged motions,
pal-ing up with him, ever his companion
in doorways, around corners,
in crowds, between tables—
always eager for people around
to know they are a pair,
he's directed the wife to be vigilant,
industrious, patient, and strong.
She's to lift and stoop,
write bills, letters,
keep the calendar, cook, and clean.
He's warned her to be ready
to sacrifice a schedule,
an independent thought.
He's told her to keep up conversations,
trained her in medication dispensing.
She's to be ready for falls, indigestion,
evenings of silence.

VIII.
They're holding out hope
that someday, someone
smart and great will come
to take away their guest.
He's become the cart before the horse,
The Man Who Came to Dinner,
The bass ackards
of their lives.

Forced Laughter

In the literature, which is much,
and claims a section in our file cabinet,
the Parkinsonians are smiling greedily,
even laughing, their heads tossed back,
teeth gleaming, dimples showing.
They wade the surf with grandchildren,
or lean to lovers on the decks of cruise ships,
ready to go inside and dance the night away.
They are quilting, playing Santa, woodworking,
grooming dogs, baking cakes, and sailing.
A whole subset lies in the grass, head
in the lap of the other. Always sun and wind
treat them well, and their dentures are holding.
In fact, they are so happy one would think the world
would be a better place if everyone had Parkinson's.

Gait Initiation Syndrome

Even the longest journey must begin
where you stand.
                    —Lao-Tzu

When you stall out forward, you're to
take a step backward, then move ahead.
Think of it like cranking a Model T,
or an outfielder going for a high ball,
a skate boarder gaining momentum,
or rocking one-way in an old porch chair.
People stare. What is he doing?
Evil Knieveling your errant brain,
you slow-dance with Parkinson.

Key Ceremony
(after the fender-bender)

"Don't say a word," you say.
I wasn't about to.
"Hold out your hand."
I do.
"Here are my keys."
I take them.
"Doing this my way—"
I nod
"—not the highway."

Faces in Everything

Lately, he's been seeing faces—
the side of the spoon rack,
the quilt early morning,
rain leaks on the ceiling tiles—
they're all folks.

Outdoors is not immune either—
visages in the shrubbery,
a little girl in the hibiscus,
a gnome peering out of the birdbath,
the oak glaring from across the street.

He does not tell her all—
too many, he says, and besides,
it would scare her:
the hordes they fly through 5 miles up,
the crowds she's entertaining in their house,
the ladies taking a bath with him.

Obsessions

The info says there may be obsessions,
like gambling, sex, or creativity.
You have chosen the latter,
so we have objects from palm trees:
spears, obelisks, stylized cacti,
a badger and parrot, mobile-floating fish,
a golden lizard scampering up the wall,
butterflies handsome but earthbound:
paint, sequins, string, and glue.

Now there is drawing in pencil—
portraits of grandchildren,
your mother and father,
your saxophone,
your childhood dog Zero,
and a cartooned senior
in Superman costume.

PROGRESSION

Happy he who learns to bear what he cannot change.
—Friedrich Schiller
(1759-1805)

Part-time

Mornings you can talk,
forget your cane,
proceed with life,
watering your tomatoes,
mucking the compost,
picking limes.

Afternoons you stumble—
feet and speech left
behind in the yard,
your blue eyes
reflecting other than sky.

"What the hell are you doing?"
you ask your hands.
"Where do you think you're going?"
you ask your nose, now running,
your feet marching in place.

"This is not my shift,"
your body replies.
"Don't you remember?
I get off at noon.
See you tomorrow—
we can argue again then."

Prey and Predator

Before Parkinson's,
he never knew thresholds could lurk,
cafe tables form herds across his plains,
pews at church gather in unholy rows.
He never considered steps rapacious,
steep inclines or declines poisonous,
holes in the lawn to be stalkers,
extension cords and rugs in disguise.
Now there are venomous tile floors,
the wily smiles of shining lobbies,
man-eating sidewalks, spidery chairs,
the distance between here and there
waiting in ambush.

Slogans

"Whatever!" tops our list.
A runner-up: "It is what it is."
And the 12-step folks remind,
"One day at a time."

The short answers to
"How are you?"—
"Okay."
"Fair to middlin'."
"So-so."
"Up and around."
And one that makes us smile,
old Uncle Buddy's reply,
"Well, I'm able to sit up
and take nourishment."

Freezing

It is illogical, counter-intuitive:
this "freezing" you do today,
a day with mercury in the 90's,
no rain expected. It is,
as we children once said,
No fair, King's X.
You have clamored from the car,
and now framed in a doorway,
you stand inches from a chair,
synapses wandering like lost octopi,
waiting for a little magic juice
to speed them on their way.
Remember "Slinging Statue"
we played as children?
It was fun, this freezing in position
where we were slung.
The first one who moved was It.
Oh, for you to be It again!

Hypomimia

"Mask-like expression" it's kindly put
by the literature: a lack
of facial tone hiding age, intention,
pain, delight, and all between.

Stumbling on an album photo
of you at sixteen, I revel in
your parted lips, your teeth,
your lit eyes, your slight dimples.

Today you are my Greek drama,
archaic vizard, masquerade,
your face lending your thoughts
to my imagination.

Threshold Initiation Syndrome

Like a cat, you pause before a doorway,
ancient limbic cells deep in your brain
working overtime with the signal
Caution! Beware! New territory!

Strangers kind to a fault insist
on holding public doors for you—
you standing frantic, looking at
your disobedient feet.

Finally, neurons fire, synapses
snap to, jambs unjam and you
pass from room to room,
sidewalk to café, yard to house.

If you had your way, you'd prefer
not to fight these Threshold Wars.
The victories are monotonous.

Night Sweats

They aren't kind, these rainforests of the body,
mini-monsoons taking over your bed at 3 a.m.
"We're here to rain on the parade you weren't having anyway."
Bringing dry pajamas and sheets, I recall my mother
doing the same for me, a child of six with tuberculosis.
She'd raise me up to see my angel-in-the-snow imprint,
spread the sunshine-smelling new sheet, deftly slip off
my "sopping wet" gown, replace it with another, cool and dry.
I will not recount all this in the middle of the night,
both of us sleep-drunk, ready to return to restless dreaming.
But come morning I will tell you that I am not an impassive caregiver,
that I have been the recipient of the love I now give you,
not just love but what is meant by the practice of love.
I will tell you that I know what it means to be clean and dry,
to lie smoothed, to start over, in hope, the second half of a night.

You and Turtles

They say owners come to resemble their pets.
Or do people pick pets which look like them?
Whichever, you have succeeded, favoring
the land tortoises and pond sliders
migrating to us and our backyard via the gate
or friends moving to no-pet places.
There was Bessie, who could not get enough
of your male charm, underfoot wherever you went,
even following you past the door of your shop.
And Surprise who, adopting our small pond,
surfaced at your claps to eat shrimp from your hand.
You've absorbed their abilities: perfected "slow,"
the hokey-poke-along, stop and go,
the sudden hustle away from danger. Silence.
More than once, you've been found on your back,
but helped to turn over, proceeded your stoical way.
Indifferent to heat or cold, you are quick to withdraw
from noise and light. You prefer fruit for supper.
Inside your shell patterned by a lifetime of work
is soul-flesh, thought after inscrutable thought,
stillness, wary waiting, old earth wisdom.

TREATMENT

*Extreme remedies are very appropriate for
extreme diseases.*
—Hippocrates
(400 B.C.)

Dear Dr. Parkinson

I am writing you this letter some two centuries later
to offer thanks for lending your name to a disease.
It's not often someone gives up his good name
to a mysterious, miserable, long-lasting ailment.
It probably wasn't easy, when they asked you,
or did they ask you? You must have wondered
whether you were worthy of the honor
since you based "An Essay on the Shaking Palsy"
on six patients, one of which you only glanced at
across the street and another who moved away.
Still you earned the right with your monograph.
We never know, do we, what will make us famous?
You wrote also about fossils, politics, and lightning.
Just think: Students could be writing your name
into their exams: Tyrannosaurus Parkinsonus,
Parkinson's Law, or The Parkinson Cloud Effect.
I'm guessing you would rather have
lent your name to a star, a flower, or a bird.

Granted you're in fine company, a little club all your own
with Doctors Alzheimer, Asperger, Tourette,
Graves, Downs, and Huntington.
Here's another advantage: you have your name
on institutes, clinics, laboratories, endowments, support
groups, newsletters, dinners, races, and tee shirts.

So I'm just reaching back in time to 1817,
when you wrote in such an explicit and significant way
about a disease that had so befuddled the ancients
that none was able to get a handle on it for 2,000 years.

By the way, I have to say that in our household,
your name is mentioned many more times a day

than is Christ, Hitler, Buddha, and Churchill combined.

Thank you, James. (I'm calling you that, being familiar
just this once so you'll know there's someone
out there that thinks of you other than a disease.)

Yours truly

The Words Are Not the Thing

Hypothalamus and Hippocampus
might have been twin Greek gods
who lived in the globus pallidus.

Meanwhile, descriptions of movements
sound like horse training:
halting gait, stutter steps, threshold hesitancy.

Then there's the splat of dysautonomia,
the tongue-twisting amygdala,
the possibly offensive substantia nigra.

These are offset by the mellifluous levodopa,
festination, and nocturnal myoclonus.
A famous poet, often quoted, said,

"What we cannot name, we do not understand."
Not so. We can name these names
but we will never understand.

The Short of It

There once lived in your brain dopamine
whose scarcity now is obscene.
Substantia nigra cells
are the ones raising hell,
making this kind of life unforeseen.

Invitation

Oh, Dopamine, with your questionably lovely girl's name,
if only you would pull back the curtain, crack the door.
The axons are ready to send on their synaptic way.
And the dendrites are reaching, stretching.
In short, millions of cells await your juicy kiss.
Dopamine dear, won't you come out and play?

Haiku Cycle on Pills

"Medications" sounds
more Greek than "pills" can muster,
more...medicinal.

The compartments wink
open/shut like a wall of
post office boxes.

The mass is ready:
Morning, Noon, Evening, Bedtime—
you pray the stations.

Capsules and tablets
descend, then climb the steep wall
to your waiting brain.

This first-aid candy
convinces your feet to walk
and your mouth to talk.

Little prison cells
hold secrets for your escape
'til the next arrest.

Small chunks of potions,
each with its saving graces,
our graceless saving.

It's levadopa-
carbidopa time again:
twins in the belfry.

Pillows, bullets, chips
all there to do the magic
for a few more hours.

Throw them in your mouth.
Be ruthless, angry, resigned.
Miss? Now hunt them down!

The Dys-es are Dissing the Parkie

Dysphonia makes it hard to speak;
dysphagia makes it hard to eat.

Dyskinesia jerks one to and fro
where one does not wish to go.

Dystonia makes the muscles cramp;
dysarthria makes the voice decamp.

Dysphoria brings a nasty mood;
dyspraxia moves, misunderstood.

Dysergic muscles plead digression;
dyspepsia gives indigestion.

If only one could diss the dys-es,
there'd be a chance to know what bliss is.

Mnemonic

Fifteen years of neurologists.
We've gone through several—
their retirements, our travel distance;
their impatience, your impatient-cy;
their rote answers, our desperation.
We've lived hours in hushed waiting rooms,
silently comparing your health to others:
this one has tremor, that one can't walk,
this perky one's still whistling Dixie.
There's been a snow of questionnaires:
Do you drool? Have nightmares?
Have you ever lived near pesticides?
Have you ever taken recreational drugs?
Then, sudden dispensation—name called,
magazines replaced, concentration
on standing up, moving forward,
hurrying in the underwater speed of a Parkie.

It seems in the text of Neuroscience 101
there's a technique that stuck with them all.
The first visit, the doctor, it doesn't matter which, says,
"Remember these words: 'purple,' 'butterfly,' 'shoe.'
We're going to come back to them later."
Then, nearing the end of the demonstration walk,
the hands held out, the eyes up and down,
the nose-touching, the doctor demands the words.

On the latest try-out, you perform beautifully.
Posturing thought, you look down at her feet
and (no lie) what do you see?
Her purple wedges, and perched atop her
painted toenails, careful little butterflies.

The Nobility of Canes

When you first use the Medicare cane—
the J-cane, the ortho-, or the quad,
Do not let it be your bane.
Pretend you're walking like a god.

Moses, turning his staff to snake,
King Lear, fleeing sad old age,
Paul Bunyan with his walking stick,
Charles Dickens in a streetside rage;

Lady Astor with a dog's head handle,
Tenzing Norgay with a trekking pole,
Socrates in the Senate in sandals,
Falstaff tapping the stage in his role;

Shepherd with crook on Christmas night,
Mary Poppins' 'brella will be handy,
Warrior with sword cane flashing bright,
Gangster with cane for sipping brandy.

Do not walk gimpy or out of joint.
Prestige, status, momentum gain.
Clinch it, tap it, whack it, point
when you accept your Medicare cane.

Group Therapy

Today the caregivers and the caremakers
are meeting separately, and so,
like tourists on a rest stop in a forest,
the caregivers go to the right,
the Parkies to the left.

As the couples separate,
there's an almost palpable split,
caregivers looking over their shoulders,
caremakers challenging their threshold,
both groups reluctant to unglue, yet
feeling the breeze of freedom.

Here for an hour they will dump out
the boxes of their souls
and the dregs of their bodies.
The caregivers will marvel that strangers
are saying their thoughts aloud.
The Parkies will nod at their histories,
grimace at the previews.
Some will wish only for home.

When the hour is up, with reunion in the hallway,
each person will guard the frankness in recent words,
feel the guilt of new knowledge, the heart twangs.
Different in small ways,
they will greet each other with casual blank faces.
Later, reviewing the facts of common ground,
they will avoid some topics too painful to share.
For now, they exit the double doors carefully
in whatever way they can, feeling not quite alone.
Grateful. Back together.

ABIDING

*I never heard of any true affection, but 'twas nipt
with care.*
—Thomas Middleton
(1570-1627)

The Game

I am looking at you
to see if you are looking at me
looking at you, as I am waiting,
thinking whether to help you
with what you are trying to do,
which includes looking at me
to see if I am looking at you.

Evenings

We used to call it the witching hour,
this end of day when all guards were down
and raw weariness made us work to get
supper and baths and bedtime stories
for the tired, yearning children in our care.
Now it's sundown syndrome,
when we're trying to get the less charming
Parkinson kid to quit wiggling, gnawing at us,
the only bedtime story we want being rest.
We do your evening meds, designed
to hold you until dawn, secure the bandage
on the stubborn skin from your last fall.
Making sure your feet are covered to your liking,
I lean to kiss you, a flicker of remembrance
when a kiss wasn't postlude but prelude.
Your blue eyes telegraph a veiled sadness,
or just a longing to close—I can't tell which.
"Goodnight," I say, and hang there an instant
while we send each other the same message:
Be there in the morning.

Cheerfulness

Looking on the bright side,
counting the blessings,
rounding them up,
accentuating the positive
somewhere over the rainbow,
we find these plusses of Parkinson's:
handicapped parking
pre-boarding
doors opened by strangers
and that bold posting
"Handicap access."

Sleep-talking

In the next room, just beyond the wall I lie beside,
he is talking and talking, a low, slow murmur
the sense of which I cannot quite make out.

Other times he calls out, "Get off the bus!"
or "Wait!" or "You can't" clearer and louder
than he ever speaks in waking hours.

It is his story to tell, to enjoy or fret over,
to muddle through or triumph in. Come morning
he cannot say exactly how it ended.

They tell us the disease does not make distinctions
between dreaming and waking. The Parkinsonian
will speak his glossolalia, sometimes for all.

Even though I foolishly long to know him better,
this husband of many years, I am barred
at the gateway of his dreams.

His words waking me are like the light pebbles
he tossed upward at my dorm window in the days
when we loved, both dreaming and awake.

Power

Now that I drive
we're on a different journey.
Time was, I rode shotgun,
handing peppermints and threats
to a back seat writhing with boys.
Your eyes focused
the destination in your man-brain,
your hands caressed the wheel.
Now I'm awash in traffic and gasoline.
You sit beside me,
wary, propped in your pain
and mostly yearning for our driveway.
I try to imagine what it was like
to have controlled almost everything
for years and years.
For sure, I remember how I trusted,
took a catnap to the hum of the road
or your music CD.
Now you're the one saying "Watch it!"
as you brace your hand on the dash
and make that breath-sucking "sleeee!"
that you asked me for decades to desist from.
Now, if I don't talk,
try to entertain you as in old times,
I can often turn at the right place,
remember the order of our errands.
On a dark night, arriving home, and
having forgotten to turn on the porch light,
I may command,
"Get out the flashlight"—
after all, you're now
closest to the "glove department"
as one child christened it.

Yes, the flashlight—
power after I've killed the engine,
after you've labored out of your seat.
We go in, the light steady at our feet,
hanging on to a little power.

Coming to Terms

If I am the caregiver,
are you the caretaker,
that is, the receiver?
But wait—the dictionary
says a caretaker
is one who cares for another.
Okay, I know you care for me,
that you love me.
Like flammable and inflammable,
maybe we are much the same.
How about a pact:
We'll both care,
in our giving and taking,
and be careful
doing it.

Advice to a Caregiver

First will be bewilderment,
then anger, and finally, grief.
Despair will knock. Don't answer.

Learn the new language.
Your pronouns will be plural:
directives with "Let's,"
suggestions: "If I were you,"
difficulties: "We have to talk."

Assign silly names:
The disease is Sparkie.
The walker is Rolanda.
Dyskinesia is The Disser.
Take every good memory
as invitation to smile.

You will lead a double life.
"Have we taken our meds?"
"We've a doctor's appointment."
"We can't go there."

Understand that
the frown is not for you.
The worried stare
is the brain in cement shoes.
The silence is all
that can be managed.

Your life will carry you forward
like a disobedient ocean wave.
Knowing that nothing can improve
the Golden Rule as mantra,

nights you lie wide-eyed,
thinking how it must feel
to be living in that ragged body,
a thunderbolt of fate to the brain.

Now pray the release of sleep,
for you and for the other.

At 2:30 a.m.

You said later that
it was 10-15 minutes before your calls reached my tired ears.
Now, an hour more, you off the floor, things tidied,
we lie together on the hospital bed.
It's been a long time since
we had a conversation like this in the dark.
We wonder how ancient Parkinson's might be.
You say you are sorry for poor old Dr. Parkinson,
a sad distinction—a cruddy disease named after you.
I say I'm sorry for God if He invented it,
that I could be permanently mad at Him,
that I'd rather think the Devil had done it.
Then random remarks punctuated
by sleepy silences—remembering from our childhoods
this phenomenon in sleepovers—
we finally sleep, knowing only that tomorrow
will bring practical things, light to pay back this darkness,
another day of wondering.

In Bitterest Moments

Contrary to our mothers' admonitions,
times when we cannot say something
nice about Parkinson's, we cannot
not say anything. We say we'd
rather be sipping wine on a cruise ship
and soon out on the dance floor. We say
we'd rather be sharing one sleeping bag
in a northern wood after walking
on a trail all day. We'd rather only read
about Michael Fox's hot acting career.
We'd like to find "festination" a fascinating word
in the dictionary. Also, "bradykinesia."
We'd rather our grandchildren did not look on
with polite puzzled eyes. We'd be pleased
if our insurance benefits were available to needy persons.
We'd be cheered to have to hunt for
an unmarked parking space. We'd rather
the pills were Easter eggs. We'd like it if our bodies
could follow their own agendas in lovemaking.
We'd rather Jesus sent Parkinson's into the herd of swine.
We'd rather say something nice about something nice.

What You As the Parkie Have Given Me

You have given me excuses for things I did not want to do anyway.
You have given me new skills—how to fit the leg rests on a wheelchair,
how to drive a retrofitted van through city traffic,
how to organize complicated meds,
how to be grateful but brief in phrasing your health to others
who want to say they care but really only need short answers.
You have given me a fresh vocabulary of neuroscience,
a passel of new friends afloat in the same lifeboat.
And at this late date, you've given me patience I never had before,
with my strange limbic anger calmed into understanding,
with waves of resentment transformed into compassion,
and with permission to laugh with you
at things that were formerly serious and important.

About the author

Jan Seale was the 2012 Texas Poet Laureate. She and her husband Carl live in the Rio Grande Valley of Texas. They have three grown sons and four grandsons. They have lived with, marveled at, and dealt with Parkinson's Disease for twenty years.

Books by Jan Seale

Airlift
Appearances
Audie & Company
Bonds
Homeland
Jan Seale: New and Selected Poems 2013
Nape
Sharing the House
Valley Ark
The Wonder Is: New and Selected Poems 1974-2012
The Yin of It

Other Poetry from Lamar University Press

Alan Berecka, *With Our Baggage*
David Bowles, *Flower, Song, Dance: Aztec and Mayan Poetry*
Jeffrey DeLotto, *Voices Writ in Sand*
Mimi Ferebee, *Wildfires and Atmospheric Memories*
Ken Hada, *Margaritas and Redfish*
Michelle Hartman, *Disenchanted and Disgruntled*
Hoggard, Lynn, *Motherland: Stories and Poems from Louisiana*
Janet McCann, *The Crone at the Casino*
Erin Murphy, *Ancilla*
Dave Oliphant, *The Pilgrimage, Selected Poems: 1962-2012*
Carol Coffee Reposa, *Underground Musicians*

www.LamarUniversityPress.Org

CPSIA information can be obtained at www.ICGtesting.com
Printed in the USA
LVOW01s0009251113

362571LV00008BA/30/P